FAMOUS NATIVE AMERICANS™

Chief Joseph
Nez Perce Peacekeeper

Diane Shaughnessy
Jack Carpenter

The Rosen Publishing Group's
PowerKids Press™
New York

Published in 1997 by The Rosen Publishing Group, Inc.
29 East 21st Street, New York, NY 10010

First Edition

Book Design: Danielle Primiceri

Photo Credits: Cover, pp. 4, 11, 20 © Archive Photos; p. 6 © The Bettmann Archive; pp. 9, 13 © Corbis-Bettmann; p. 14 © The National Archives/Corbis; p. 15 © Medford Historical Society Collection/Corbis; pp. 18–19 © Photoworld/FPG International; p. 21 Bettmann.

Diane Shaughnessy
    Chief Joseph : Nez Perce peacekeeper / Diane Shaughnessy, Jack Carpenter.
        p.   cm. — (Famous Native Americans)
    Includes index.
    Summary: A biography of the great Nez Percé chief who, struggling desperately to keep his tribe safe and free, led them on a flight to Canada.
    ISBN 0-8239-5111-1
    1. Joseph, Nez Percé Chief, 1840–1904—Juvenile literature. 2. Nez Percé Indians—Kings and rulers—Biography—Juvenile literature. 3. Nez Percé Indians—History—Juvenile literature. [1. Joseph, Nez Percé Chief, 1840–1904. 2. Nez Percé Indians—Biography. 3. Indians of North America—Biography.] I. Carpenter, Jack, 1944-I. Title. III. Series.
E99.N5J588 1997
979'.004974'0092—dc21   97-222
                                                                              CIP
                                                                              AC

Manufactured in the United States of America

Contents

Chief Joseph

Chief Joseph is remembered as one of the greatest chiefs in Native American history. He was born in 1840 in the Wallowa Valley in what is now the state of Oregon. He belonged to the **Nez Perce** (NEZ PURS) Indians. His tribal name was Hin-mah-too-yah-lah-ket, which means "Thunder Rolling in the Mountains."

The Nez Perce lived in the Northwest. Today those areas are the states of Washington, Oregon, and Idaho.

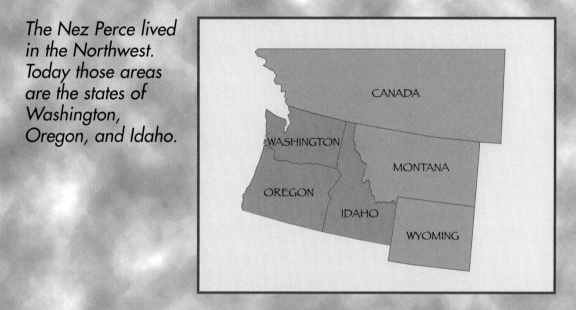

The white **traders** (TRAY-derz) living in the area called Joseph's father, the chief, Old Joseph. Old Joseph's son came to be known as Young Joseph.

◀ *Joseph's tribal name shows that his family believed in his strength and bravery.*

5

The Nez Perce

Nez Perce is French for "pierced noses." The name was given to the tribe by French fur traders. Even though few of them had pierced noses, the Nez Perce kept the name. They were peaceful Indians, often keeping to themselves. They lived in the Northwest, in what are now the states of Idaho, Washington, and Oregon. Like other Native American tribes, the Nez Perce were made up of small groups. Each group lived in its own village and had its own leader.

This painting was done by E. S. Paxson, an artist who lived in the West during the late 1800s. It shows how many Native Americans, such as the Nez Perce, worked with the traders who came to live on their land.

Nez Perce Life

The Nez Perce were hunters. They hunted deer, elk, mountain sheep, and rabbits. They fished for salmon and gathered wild plants, such as onions, carrots, and berries. They also raised horses and cattle. During the summer, they lived in teepees covered in animal **hides** (HYDZ) or in **lean-tos** (LEEN-tooz). During the winter, they made shelters by digging large pits in the ground and covering them with earth and grass.

The Nez Perce raised horses and cattle. They also hunted. ▶

Living in Peace

The Nez Perce lived in peace with white people for many years. The first white people the Nez Perce met were French fur traders in 1750. When the explorers Meriwether Lewis and William Clark traveled through their land in 1805, the Nez Perce took them in and fed them. In 1855, when Young Joseph was fifteen years old, the Nez Perce met **settlers** (SET-ul-erz) from the East. These settlers had traveled west, looking for new land to live on and farm. The Nez Perce agreed to give up part of their land. They believed that there was enough land for everyone.

The Nez Perce were very kind to Lewis and Clark, as well as other people who traveled through their land. ▶

Keeping the Peace

When Young Joseph was 23 years old, the U.S. **government** (GUH-vern-ment) tried to get several Nez Perce chiefs to give up nearly all of the tribe's land. The Nez Perce would only have had a small area, called a **reservation** (reh-zer-VAY-shun), to live on. Joseph's father and several other chiefs **refused** (ree-FYOOZD) to sign the **treaty** (TREE-tee). They continued to live in peace on their land.

Like many other tribes, the Nez Perce refused to move onto reservations.

The Flight for Freedom

Old Joseph died in 1871, and his son, Young Joseph, became chief. Around that time, white settlers began to move onto Nez Perce land without asking permission to do so. Joseph did not want to fight over the land. Twice he moved his people to avoid trouble. Then, in 1877, the

Chief Joseph didn't want to fight over land. He simply wanted his people to have the freedom to live in peace on their land.

government sent General Oliver Howard and his troops to move the Nez Perce to a reservation. Chief Joseph asked his people to leave quietly, and not to start a war. But his people were angry about having to leave their land. A war began. This battle is sometimes called the Flight of the Nez Perce.

The Journey

Chief Joseph met with the other Nez Perce chiefs. They agreed to leave the area. A group of 450 Nez Perce began a long **journey** (JER-nee) that lasted for seventeen weeks. Some people say the journey was 1,300 miles. Others say it was 1,700 miles. Either way, their journey took the Nez Perce from Oregon through Idaho, and into Montana, toward the Canadian border. They fought in thirteen battles along the way.

◀ *Chief Joseph led his people on a journey from Oregon toward Canada in search of freedom.*

More Soldiers

Three armies of soldiers chased the Nez Perce on their journey. The government sent its best generals to lead the armies. One of them was General Howard. But Chief Joseph, other tribal chiefs, and warriors were able to fight these armies and escape.

The Nez Perce warriors were good, smart fighters. They were able to fight off the soldiers in nearly every battle. ▶

There were nearly 2,000 soldiers in each battle. There were only 250 Nez Perce **warriors** (WAR-ee-yurz). But the Nez Perce warriors won nearly every battle. People all over the country admired the skill and **courage** (KER-ej) of Chief Joseph and his warriors.

The Last Fight

On September 29th, 1877, less than 40 miles from the Canadian border, Chief Joseph felt safe enough to slow down the march. He wanted to let his people rest and to take care of those who were hurt. But General Nelson Miles and his army attacked them the next morning. Surrounded

Although he captured Chief Joseph and his people, General Miles promised they could return to their homeland.

Chief Joseph fought hard for his people. But he knew it was time for everyone to stop fighting. ▶

by his people, many of whom were hurt and hungry, Chief Joseph said, "Hear me, my chiefs! I am tired. My heart is sick and sad. From where the sun now stands, I will fight no more forever." Then Chief Joseph **surrendered** (ser-EN-derd) to the soldiers.

21

A Broken Heart

General Miles promised to let Chief Joseph and his people return to their land. But the U.S. government broke that promise. The Nez Perce were forced to live on a reservation in Oklahoma. Finally, in 1885, the Nez Perce were allowed to move back to reservations on their homeland. When Chief Joseph died in 1904, the doctor on the reservation said that he died of a broken heart. Chief Joseph's strength, courage, honesty, and wisdom had made him a great leader. Chief Joseph helped to save his people by knowing when to stop fighting.

Glossary

courage (KER-ej) Bravery.

government (GUH-vern-ment) The people who lead a country.

hide (HYD) An animal skin.

journey (JER-nee) A long trip from one place to another.

lean-to (LEEN-too) A shelter built against something, such as a tree, that is usually open on one side.

Nez Perce (NEZ PURS) A Native American tribe.

refuse (ree-FYOOZ) To say no to.

reservation (reh-zer-VAY-shun) An area of land set aside by the government for the Native Americans to live on.

settler (SET-ul-er) A person who sets up house in a new place.

surrender (ser-EN-der) To give up.

trader (TRAY-der) A person who exchanges goods for money or other goods.

treaty (TREE-tee) An agreement between two groups of people.

warrior (WAR-ee-yur) A person who fights battles.

Index